# CHEMICAL WEAPONS AND WESTERN SECURITY POLICY

## The Aspen Strategy Group and The European Strategy Group

in cooperation with
the Aspen Institute Berlin

Published by
The Aspen Strategy Group
and
University Press of America

**Copyright © 1987 by**

**The Aspen Institute for Humanistic Studies**

**University Press of America,® Inc.**

4720 Boston Way
Lanham, MD 20706

3 Henrietta Street
London WC2E 8LU England

Printed in the United States of America

**Library of Congress Cataloging-in-Publication Data**

Chemical weapons and Western security policy.

  "Co-published by arrangement with the Aspen Institute
for Humanistic Studies"—T.p. verso.
  Papers presented at a workshop for members of the
Aspen Strategy Group and the European Strategy Group,
held at the Aspen Institute Berlin, June 12-14, 1986
  Bibliography: p.
  1. North Atlantic Treaty Organization—Congresses.
2. Chemical warfare—Congresses.  I. Aspen Strategy
Group (U.S.)  II. European Strategy Group.  III. Aspen
Institute Berlin.
US646.3.C49   1987      358'.34      87-1987
ISBN 0-8191-6169-1 (alk. paper)
ISBN 0-8191-6170-5 (pbk. : alk. paper)

Co-published by arrangement with
The Aspen Institute for Humanistic Studies

The Aspen Institute for Humanistic Studies and its logo
are trademarks of The Aspen Institute for Humanistic Studies.

*m.R.* *Cover Design: Edmund Lyon*

All University Press of America books are produced on acid-free
paper which exceeds the minimum standards set by the National
Historical Publication and Records Commission.

# The Aspen Strategy Group

The Aspen Strategy Group is a bipartisan committee organized under the auspices of the Aspen Institute for Humanistic Studies. The Group's primary goal is to help advance thinking and practice in the areas of international security and East-West relations. It aims to relate differing perspectives about the long-term direction of American security to current policy debates. As a standing body, the Group acts as a source of private policy advice; it contributes to the public debate through reports and other publications; and it encourages the study of broad conceptual issues that shape security but which are sometimes hurried over in debates regarding immediate policy choices.

# The European Strategy Group

The European Strategy Group was established in 1985 to provide a framework for collaborative research efforts on European security, Atlantic affairs, and East-West relations. The Group brings together senior experts from a variety of disciplines, nationalities, and research institutions in the fields of foreign and defense policy studies. It aims to initiate and coordinate major research efforts that no individual institute would be in a position to undertake. Its work includes both the study of broad strategic concepts and assessment of current policy issues. The Group currently has members from France, Italy, Norway, West Germany, and the United Kingdom.

**Members**

*Pierre Hassner,* Fondation Nationale des Sciences Politiques (FNSP), Paris, France

*Johan Holst (currently on leave),* Norsk Utenrikspolitisk Institutt (NUPI) Oslo, Norway

*Karl Kaiser,* Forschungsinstitut der Deutschen Gesellschaft für Auswärtige Politik (DGAP), Bonn, West Germany

*Laurence Martin,* Newcastle University, Newcastle upon Tyne, United Kingdom

*Sir Ronald Mason,* Hunting Engineering Ltd., Ampthill, Bedford, United Kingdom

*Thierry de Montbrial,* Institut Français des Relations Internationales (IFRI), Paris, France

*Uwe Nerlich (Chairman),* Stiftung Wissenschaft und Politik (SWP), Ebenhausen, West Germany

*John Roper,* Royal Institute of International Affairs (RIIA), London, United Kingdom

*Stefano Silvestri,* Istituto Affari Internazionali (IAI), Rome, Italy

**Executive Secretary**

*Holger Mey,* Stiftung Wissenshaft und Politik (SWP), Ebenhausen, West Germany

# CONTENTS

# ABOUT THIS REPORT

This report is the first in a series of joint studies undertaken by the Aspen Strategy Group and the European Strategy Group.

The Aspen Strategy Group is a program of the Aspen Institute for Humanistic Studies. As a bipartisan committee, the Group aims to relate differing perspectives about the long-term direction of international security to current policy debates in the United States. The European Strategy Group is a coordinating body with members from major European national institutes in the field of foreign and security policy studies. It aims to foster dialogue and cooperative research endeavors both within Europe and between Europe and America on issues of common security concern.

This report is the product of a joint study committee composed of individuals representing the two groups. The committee convened a workshop on "Chemical Weapons and European Security," on June 12–14, 1986 at the Aspen Institute Berlin. The U.S. cochairman is Joseph S. Nye, and U.S. members include: Antonia Handler Chayes, Paul Doty, Karen E. House, Walter Slocombe, and John Steinbruner. James A. Schear is the U.S. rapporteur. The European cochairman is Uwe Nerlich, and European members include: Pierre Hassner, Karl Kaiser, Laurence Martin, Thierry de Montbrial, and John Roper. Holger Mey is the European rapporteur.

Generous support for this project was provided by the Carnegie Corporation of New York, the Ford Foundation, the MacArthur Foundation, the Rockefeller Foundation, and the Volkswagen Foundation. The joint committee is also very grateful to Shepard Stone, Daniel Hamilton, and the staff of the Aspen Institute Berlin for their hospitality and support during the workshop in Berlin.

Guests of the joint study committee at the workshop included the following individuals: Benoit d'Aboville, David Anderson, Markus Berger, Col. Bruno de Blanpré, Sheila Buckley, Theodore Gold, Elisa Harris, Joachim Krause, Gen. Frederick Kroesen, Jean-Yves Leloup, Col. James E. Leonard, Sir Ronald Mason, Matthew Meselson, Robert Mikulak, A. J. J. Ooms, Michael Pakenham, Julian Perry Robinson, Enid Schoettle, K. -Peter Stratmann, Stefano Silvestri, Amb. Friedrich Ruth, and Col. Klaus Wiesmann. We are very grateful for their participation and contributions. We also owe a special debt to those who prepared background papers for the workshop: Theodore Gold, Elisa Harris, Joachim Krause, Gen. Frederick Kroesen, Matthew Meselsen, and Julian Perry Robinson. Finally, we want to thank Ann Callahan, Maude Fish, and Julie de Preux for their assistance in the editing and preparation of the manuscript.

Readers should take careful note that the contents of this report are the sole responsibility of the members of the joint study committee. Guests at the workshop, other members of the two groups, and funding or sponsoring organizations are not responsible for the views or opinions expressed in this report.

# _____ EXECUTIVE SUMMARY

Chemical weapons pose a major policy challenge to the United States and its NATO allies. Moral objection to chemical warfare (CW) is widespread in the alliance. In the absence of a total ban on chemical weapons, the alliance has sought to deter the Soviet Union from engaging in CW in the event of conflict. NATO's deterrence posture relies in part on retaliatory capability possessed by the United States; on protective measures to enable Western troops to fight in a chemically contaminated environment; and, perhaps most fundamentally, on nuclear deterrence. It is widely understood that use of CW by the Soviet Union might represent such a grave escalation of a conflict as to compel NATO to consider the use of nuclear weapons in response.

NATO's present policies are clouded with uncertainty. Perceptions of a growing disparity between NATO and Warsaw Pact CW capabilities have prompted the alliance to consider modernizing its defensive posture as well as the U.S. arsenal. Meanwhile, the stationing of U.S. chemical weapons in the Federal Republic of Germany (where a small portion of stocks is now stored) has become increasingly controversial. In May 1986, as part of an effort to

ix

gain NATO endorsement of U.S. plans to acquire new chemical weapons, President Reagan agreed to withdraw existing stocks and not to station new ones in Europe short of a crisis or a wartime situation in which responsible governments agreed that redeployment was necessary. This action is seen by many observers as neutralizing NATO's chemical deterrent since weapons stockpiled thousands of miles away and lacking priority to be shipped might have little deterrent effect.

The prospects of a comprehensive chemical weapons ban remain uncertain. While some disagreements at the talks have been narrowed in recent years, the principal actors remain at odds over key verification issues. Meanwhile, CW capabilities are spreading. Twenty years ago, only about half a dozen countries possessed chemical weapons; that number, according to some estimates, has now risen to sixteen. Repeated chemical attacks by Iraq on Iranian forces in the Gulf War provide dramatic evidence that established taboos against CW are breaking down. Against this background, there is growing disagreement among experts over the plausibility of a comprehensive ban and the relative worth of alternate arms control approaches.

## 1. CHEMICAL WEAPONS AND THE CHALLENGE TO NATO

Chemical weapons are relegated to a specialized role in NATO strategy: to deter the first use of CW by the other side once conflict has begun. Under NATO's rules of engagement, member countries possessing chemical weapons would refrain from using them, even if it were militarily advantageous to do, unless or until the Warsaw Pact struck first. This *"no-first-use"* policy is broadly consistent with customary international law as codified by the 1925 Geneva Protocol. The controversial issue is: how best to deter the Warsaw Pact? Debates on CW, which pivot ostensibly on whether one is "for" or "against" new chemical weapons, are very often disagreements about deterrence requirements.

The military value of chemical weapons is their ability to disrupt an adversary's combat operations. CW could be used to produce panic or casualties among unprotected troops, to force the other side into a cumbersome defensive posture, or to deny easy use of key facilities, like airfields, ports, or supply depots. The major drawbacks of chemical weapons are their sensitivity to topographical characteristics or weather conditions in the target area; their potential for area effects and civilian casualties that are hard to control due to downwind drift; and, in certain scenarios, their unfavorable comparison to high explosive (HE) munitions in terms of lethal effect once the other side has "suited up" with protective clothing.

Numerous individual defensive measures (gas mask, overgarments, etc.) and collective measures (air-filtration systems, shelters, alarm and decontamination systems, etc.) are available to reduce the lethal effects of CW, but all pose some penalty on combat efficiency. In coping with a chemical threat, field commanders would face difficult trade-offs between assuring protection of troops against CW attacks and maintaining the performance of the military unit as a whole. Too much protection can be self-defeating. Some heightened degree of exposure to the risks of CW may be necessary to avoid casualties or defeat, stemming from a loss of one's overall position on the battlefield.

New technologies are being pursued that could substantially augment CW offensive and defensive capabilities. More accurate delivery systems, better dispersal techniques, and "binary" weapons design (in which the constituent chemicals are not lethally toxic until mixed just prior to delivery on the target) are the key offensive developments. More transportable and reliable alarm sys-

tems, higher quality protective gear, and better intelligence systems (to enable troops to operate at lower levels
of protection without getting caught off guard) are in
prospect on the defensive side. A special source of concern is new biotechnologies for production of genetically
engineered toxins, which might be easy to proliferate and
hard to detect on the battlefield. But not enough is known
to form hard conclusions on their potential. If our intelligence is adequate to the task of warning about threatening
developments, it seems improbable that new technology
per se would alter the current offense/defense balance in
any significant way.

How important is the CW option for the Soviet Union
and its Pact allies? The Soviets appear well trained and
equipped to engage in chemical warfare. The Soviet investment in protective CW measures exceeds comparable
Western programs. While our knowledge of Soviet offensive capabilities is sketchy, Soviet CW stocks are thought
to be quite diverse. The number of their CW-capable
delivery systems, especially short-range missiles, is particularly striking. Even so, the operational significance of
this posture and plausible Soviet incentives for using CW
are the subjects of much debate.

Many Western experts believe that current Soviet planning places great importance on a nonnuclear, high speed
conventional offensive, in which Soviet forces would attempt to achieve major breakthroughs without nuclear
weapons while preempting NATO's option to escalate.
Some observers argue that the Soviets see CW as a decisive substitute for nuclear weapons. They argue that the
Pact would use chemically tipped short-range ballistic
missiles (SRBMs) in a "quasi-strategic" mode against rear
targets like airfields and engage NATO ground forces with
selective (or massive localized) attacks closer to the forward edge of battle. Critics of this view say that claims of
heavy Soviet reliance on CW are greatly exaggerated.
These observers argue that tactical use of CW against

not be necessary if CW were too impractical to be useful. The reality lies somewhere in between.

—Choices regarding CW posture should be sensitive to the criterion of *operational effectiveness*. Special attention should be paid to the trade-offs between HE munitions and CW against the same set of targets. Chemical weapons are not likely to enhance deterrence if their relative costs of delivery are high and if they are perceived as displacing HE munitions that could have more enduring destructive effects.

These considerations suggest a balanced approach to maintaining CW deterrence. First, they underscore the importance of *further improving NATO's defensive posture.* Defensive measures contribute to NATO's fighting flexibility and thus to the specialized form of deterrence at stake with chemical weapons. They also provide a unique form of deterrence that weapons cannot match: if NATO had no defenses, Pact commanders might well conclude that triggering retaliation in kind was a small price to pay for the option of devastating unprotected forces with chemical attacks. NATO's investment should be targeted to specific needs: greater research into the nature of combat degradation imposed by protective gear, more advanced detection systems that identify the type of agent being used and give an "all clear" signal, and better collective protection, training, and decontamination. Priority should be given to defensive technologies that enable forces to respond flexibly to changing levels of threat.

Second, NATO should give greater attention to *"non-CW" initiatives* that might improve the robustness of NATO's defensive posture. Improved tactical communications, for instance, would alert field commanders to the use of CW in adjoining sectors and thus allow them to make more informed judgments on defensive readiness. In addition, anti-tactical ballistic missiles (ATBMs) might

discourage Soviet efforts to engage in deep strike attacks.
Such measures contribute in a general way to NATO's
overall conventional capabilities. For this reason, they
must be justified in large part on the basis of needs
outside the CW area. But their contribution to CW deterrence is also important.

Third, there is the question of the *retaliatory component*
of NATO's posture. Nuclear weapons unavoidably play a
role in deterrence: if Soviet use of CW were seen as the
pivotal factor in turning the tide of battle against NATO,
Western leaders would face the question of deliberate
escalation in any case. Yet it is doubtful that nuclear
weapons would provide a credible form of wartime deterrence to less than massive, quasi-strategic attacks. To rely
on nuclear deterrence for this contingency would be in-
consistent with NATO's expressed intent to augment its
nonnuclear deterrent posture. Continued possession of
chemical weapons is necessary in order to deny the Pact
any advantage it might gain by selectively using CW with
impunity—that is, forcing NATO troops to "suit up" without having to do so itself.

Are new chemical weapons necessary to meet this goal?
Current debate centers around the new U.S. 155 mm.
artillery shell, which will go into initial production next
year, and the *Bigeye* glide bomb, which would be delivered by fighter bombers against Pact airbases and other
fixed targets in rear areas. Proponents argue that binary
weapons would be safer to handle, more transportable,
and could be deployed in areas where peacetime storage
of existing chemicals is not permitted, like ships or airbases. They also argue that adequate deterrence requires
the capability to retaliate to Pact use on the level that it
occurs—potentially, throughout the depth of the theater
of operations. Opponents of binary weapons reply that
there are already sufficient numbers of artillery shells
available for short-range retaliation and that the requirement for a long-range attack option is open to question.

deterrence. However, the obstacles are considerable: chemical weapons are not easy to count or to characterize with national technical means of verification; their delivery systems are diverse; the industrial capacity to produce lethal chemicals is widely distributed throughout the economies of all industrial countries; and broad multilateral adherence to a CW ban is not a foregone conclusion, even if Washington and Moscow could work out a consensus approach. All these factors make a CW ban hard to define, to negotiate, and, if achieved, to verify.

Current restraints, based largely on the 1925 Geneva Protocol and the 1972 Biological Weapons Convention (BWC), ban the use—but not retaliatory use for some countries—of chemical weapons and the possession, stockpiling, transfer, and use of biological weapons. This regime is being stressed under a growing number of problems. The taboos against first use are eroding as the number of countries armed with chemical weapons increases. Compliance standards in parts of the BWC and the Protocol are not well defined, and the United States has charged the Soviet Union with violations of both agreements. In addition, the BWC is not verifiable. Biological weapons were widely viewed as having so little military value that no real verification was deemed necessary at the time.

Negotiations on a comprehensive ban, which began initially as bilateral discussions in 1977, have been painstaking. There is broad agreement on the scope of a ban, and that existing stockpiles and production facilities would be declared promptly and destroyed within ten years. In addition, the Soviets now accept that the destruction procedures could be monitored *continuously* by an on-site inspection (OSI) procedure, and they appear to be moving toward a quota of OSIs to verify the nondiversion of civil production means to military uses. These are important developments. However, both sides remain at odds over other issues, including the proper role of "challenge" OSIs. In a hardening of its previous position, the United States now insists on a short-notice (48 hour) mandatory challenge procedure that would allow U.S. or Soviet inspectors to check into possible noncompliance anywhere on national territory. The Soviets reject anything more substantial than voluntary inspections.

It is fair to ask how much more progress can reasonably be expected in the near term. The problems associated with undeclared stocks and production would be extremely difficult to resolve, even with unprecedented access to national territory. The security goal of denying the Soviets a well-honed offensive CW capability could probably be achieved without high confidence verification because the testing and exercising of such a capability is much harder to hide than violations of the possession ban. But verification uncertainties are politically risky. Treaties that cannot be verified with some degree of confidence risk being undermined if charges of violations—even ones without military significance—arise that cannot be disproved.

Are there more promising paths to progress? In theory, a number of alternate approaches is possible:

—*CW Nonproliferation Restraints.* CW nonproliferation is one area of possible common interest between the United States and the Soviet Union, but many countries would see a CW nonproliferation treaty (NPT) as a tactic by the superpowers to sustain their preeminence in the field. It would also tend to confer legitimacy on a number of countries—like North Korea and Syria—that reportedly already possess chemical weapons.

—*Nonzero Limitations.* An agreement specifying deep cuts but not elimination of chemical stocks might be easier to implement if small stocks were available as a hedge against undetected violations. But a nonzero threshold would also be the functional equivalent of an NPT, and the verification of nonzero limits poses its own problems.

—CW *"Free Zones."* A zone covering parts or all of Central Europe has gained popularity as a way to obtain Pact withdrawals in return for the presently planned removal of U.S. stocks. However, many West Germans object to special status arrangements that would tend to divide their country from the rest of the alliance, and any move to redeploy weapons in a crisis (or as a response to Soviet violations) could embroil the alliance in a debate over treaty compliance. Verification would also be very difficult.

Clearly, none of these partial steps can match a total, verifiable ban in terms of the range of constraining effects. Some oppose these measures on the grounds that they would draw attention away from a total ban and open the way for further modernization of chemical arsenals. But other experts warn that if the international community holds out for a total ban, it may end up with nothing, which would suit only those who oppose arms control in principle.

In light of these problems, two options should be considered. *First,* it is worth looking outside the realm of formal agreements to advance the goals of CW restraint. For example, a more productive way to address proliferation might be further development of a "suppliers group" approach, in which members would pool intelligence and attempt to coordinate export controls. While effective export constraint would be harder to achieve than it is in the nuclear area, such a group would help to broaden international awareness of, and coordinate measures against, countries attempting to acquire CW. *Second,* it may be possible to exploit areas of overlap between partial steps and a total ban. For instance, a nonzero limit could be negotiated as part of a phased agreement leading toward a total ban.

# 4. CONCLUSIONS

In thinking through the problems of managing the chemical weapons issue, some basic points should be kept in mind:

1. *Chemical weaponry is a sensitive issue, but it is a second order issue compared to the importance of alliance unity in deterring a conventional or nuclear war in Europe.* Controversy over modernization or deployment of chemical weapons should not be allowed to place political burdens on the alliance such as those that arose in recent debates over the deployment of intermediate-range nuclear weapons in Europe. The damage that disunity would do to deterrence would far outweigh the gains from optimal rather than less satisfactory military solutions to the deployment of chemical weapons.

2. *Given the importance of raising the nuclear threshold as well as deterring any war, few believe that NATO policy should allow nuclear deterrence to be the only means of deterring a chemical attack.* Nuclear deterrence is fundamental to preserving the peace in Europe, but in a wartime situation, in which the dividing line between war and peace had been crossed, the idea of threatening nuclear retaliation to selective chemical attack may not be viewed as credible.

3. *The merits of the NATO decision to modernize chemical weapons while removing them from Europe in peacetime are highly debatable.* The missing ingredient in NATO policy is an allied consensus that some chemical weapons have to be based in Europe in order to deter Soviet CW use. If a reversal of the decision to withdraw existing stocks were possible, it would be desirable. At the same time, the decision has created a new political reality. It is not true that there is no deterrent value in weapons deployed outside of Europe. NATO needs to devote attention to making sure that the capacity exists

to redeploy chemical weapons to forward areas on a timely basis.

4. *It is a mistake to exaggerate the Soviet chemical threat and to assume that NATO should have similar capabilities either in the quantity or type of stockpile.* There is no operational or deterrent justification for NATO to acquire a large-scale warfighting capability. Nuclear weapons and conventional forces are much more fundamental to deterrence of aggression in Europe; it is short-sighted to think that chemical weapons would be a good substitute for either. With a modest and mobile retaliatory force and a robust program of defensive measures, NATO's aim should be to deter selective use of CW and to ensure protection against CW attacks with a minimum of disruption.

5. *The issue of binary weapons has become an overly simple litmus test that draws attention away from other important questions.* While many, though not all, of those involved in this report believe that some modernization of the chemical stockpile is prudent, including a modest amount of longer range systems, a number are skeptical about current plans for the acquisition of binary shells and bombs. Some see binary weapons as conceptually sound, while others doubt that the benefits of binaries outweigh the costs. Modernization issues should not be allowed to draw attention away from the importance of defensive measures as an aspect of deterrence in the chemical area.

6. *Chemical arms control should be accorded a higher priority in current negotiations, but one need not hold out for achievement of a total ban in order to obtain progress.* The prospects of near-term breakthroughs on a total ban are unlikely. Partial arms control approaches sacrifice a degree of comprehensiveness, but may offer greater payoff in terms of progress in the near term, provided they are seen as steps on the road to a total ban. Fortunately, the oft-cited contradiction between mod-

ernization and disarmament is not as sharp as is often made out. Modernization could result in smaller stockpiles than exist today, and determination to acquire new weapons will arguably improve the Western negotiating posture.

It bears repeating that NATO would be far better off if both sides dispensed with chemical weapons in the long run. Only time will tell whether this judgment can be translated into widespread agreement on a durable ban. Soviet leaders may calculate that disarray within NATO on CW would work to their interests. Current trends suggest that they may not need to negotiate an agreement to achieve substantial disarmament on the Western side. On the other hand, their assessment might change if they reckoned that, in a wartime situation, their own first use of chemicals would force them to prepare for a chemical response or a substantial escalation of conflict. In that circumstance, they might well conclude that chemicals were not worth the costs, and that the time had come to accelerate cooperation toward the ultimate goal of a total ban.

# INTRODUCTION

Throughout the twentieth century chemical warfare (CW) has borne an odious stigma. Memories of poison gas clouds drifting across the battlefields of Europe more than seventy years ago live on as the ultimate horror of the first World War. CW is universally regarded as a dirty, undignified form of combat—something to be prevented or banned if possible. Any significant use of modern chemical agents in wartime would pose enormous risk to civilian populations, not only in absolute terms but relative to the much smaller scale of harm inflicted upon protected troops on the battlefield. For these reasons, moral objection to CW is both widespread and profound.[1]

Within the NATO alliance, the CW issue has always been treated with great caution. In the absence of a comprehensive and verifiable ban on chemical weapons, which is strongly supported throughout the alliance, member states have sought an effective means to dissuade the Warsaw Pact from engaging in chemical attacks if war were to break out. The Western posture is based in part on the threat of retaliation in kind. The alliance relies for deterrence on the chemical arsenal of the United States. A small portion of U.S. weapons are currently stored in the Federal Republic of Germany.[2] In addition, most NATO members have invested in CW defensive measures (e.g., gas masks, protective clothing, detection systems) to provide their troops with some degree of capability to operate

1

in a chemically contaminated environment; defensive measures are an essential part of a deterrent capability. Nuclear deterrence is another, more fundamental ingredient in NATO's overall effort to forestall the other side's use of CW. It is widely understood within the alliance that any use of CW by the Soviet Union might represent such a grave escalation of conflict as to compel NATO to consider the use of nuclear weapons in response.

Although NATO's approach to CW has received general support over the years, the current situation is clouded with uncertainty. Perceptions of a growing disparity between NATO and Warsaw Pact CW capabilities have increasingly forced the alliance to address the issue of modernizing the U.S. chemical stockpile as well as its defensive posture. The Reagan Administration has advocated a program to acquire new chemical weapons while phasing out older stocks. During May 1986, in an effort to gain NATO endorsement of U.S. plans, as required by the U.S. Congress, President Reagan agreed to withdraw existing CW stocks from the Federal Republic by 1992 and not to station new ones there short of a crisis or wartime situation in which responsible governments agreed that redeployment was necessary. This action has been interpreted by many observers as neutralizing NATO's chemical deterrent since weapons stockpiled thousands of miles away and lacking the priority to be shipped in time of crisis might have little deterrent effect.

The modernization issue is only part of a broader range of problems in the CW area. Progress toward a comprehensive ban, which would obviate the need for new weapons, remains elusive. While some positive steps have been taken at the negotiations in recent years, the United States, the Soviet Union, and other key actors remain at odds over key verification issues. Meanwhile, CW capabilities are spreading. Twenty years ago, only about half a dozen countries possessed chemical weapons; that number reportedly has now risen to sixteen.[3] CW is seen by some as a cheap way to acquire a mass destruction capability. Repeated chemical attacks by Iraq on Iranian forces in the Gulf War provide dramatic evidence that established taboos against the use of CW are breaking down.

All these trends—growing debate over new CW weapons, uncertainty about arms control, and the threat of proliferation—pose problems for the alliance. The consensus over CW is fragile. While very few in NATO argue for unilateral disarmament in the face of a CW threat from the Warsaw Pact, there is widespread debate over what kind of military posture is required to deter it. Similarly, while very few would deny the virtues of a durable ban on CW, there are disagreements over the plausibility of such a goal and the relative worth of alternate arms control approaches, especially as the trend toward greater proliferation continues.

This report lays out the major issues at stake in NATO's chemical weapons policy and attempts to weigh the implications of various policy options. No analysis in the space of a few pages can purport to be a comprehensive treatment of the subject; nor is it our aim to advocate a single set of policy judgments. Our aim is to clarify three critical issues. The first is the nature of the threat. How useful are chemicals in wartime and how significant are Warsaw Pact capabilities? The second is the range and plausibility of NATO's responses. What does effective deterrence of chemical attacks require? The third issue is CW arms control. How troublesome are the present obstacles to a ban on chemical stockpiles? Are there other useful avenues for achieving progress?

# 1

# CHEMICAL WEAPONS AND THE CHALLENGE TO NATO

The Western alliance deliberately treats chemical weapons as a special class of munition. Unlike nuclear or conventional forces, which provide the bulwark of deterrence to aggression in Europe, NATO strategy relegates CW to a specific wartime role: *to deter the first use of chemicals* by the Warsaw Pact once conflict has begun. This element of restraint is notable. Under NATO's rules of engagement, member countries possessing chemical weapons would refrain from using them, even if it were militarily advantageous to do so, unless or until the other side struck first with CW. This "no-first-use" policy is broadly consistent with the scope of customary international law that effectively bars the use of CW except in retaliation.

It is worth stressing that NATO's CW employment policy is not fundamentally a matter of dispute in the alliance—so far as is known, no responsible official has ever publicly questioned the merits of the "no-first-use" pledge. The controversial question is: what is the best way to deter Warsaw Pact use of CW? Proponents of new chemical weapons assert that the existing posture is inadequate. Not only has the threat increased, they argue, but existing U.S. weapons are mismatched to current operational tasks and cannot be launched in the same kinds of attacks—for example, on distant targets like air-bases—to which NATO is potentially vulnerable. They also point out that heavy reliance on nuclear weapons is neither credible nor wise. On the other hand, opponents of new chemical weapons reply that existing weapons provide an adequate deterrent. They also argue that CW modernization will complicate arms control negotiations, will not add much to current inhibitions on Warsaw Pact use, and will pose a large-scale threat to civilian populations.

Unfortunately, virtually all debates about CW quickly devolve to the issue of whether one is "for" or "against" new chemical weapons. In a sense, new weapons are not the real issue; deterrence is. The CW debate is being driven by divergent assumptions about deterrence that are rarely, if ever, made explicit. In order to shed some light on these underlying disagreements, this section looks at the following questions:

   —How valuable are chemicals as military instruments generally?
   —How significant are Warsaw Pact CW capabilities?

Based on this assessment, we will then turn attention in Section 2 to the questions of what options are available to NATO in coping with the threat it faces.

## *The Utility and Limitations of Chemical Weapons*

Chemical weapons exert their destructive impact through direct toxic effect on human physiology—in short, by poisoning—rather than through the kinetic force of projectiles. Most modern chemical agents are not released as "gases" but in the form of liquids, vapors, or solid aerosols. Some weapons, like nerve agents, attack the body's respiratory system and induce death within minutes; other chemical compounds, like mustard agent, while less lethal in similar doses, cause severe burns and blistering of the skin and a range of other toxic effects; still other agents, known as incapacitants, would not necessarily be lethal (except in large doses) but produce unconsciousness or hallucinations.[4] Another distinct class of chemicals falls into the category of toxins—that is, very toxic chemical substances produced by living organisms. Although their lethal effect is not transmitted in the form of disease, like biological weapons, toxins are covered under the 1972 ban on biological weapons because their method of production is essentially biological.

As battlefield weapons, the military value of chemical weapons lies less in their lethality than in their ability to disrupt or delay an adversary's combat operations. CW could be used by the attacking side to produce panic and prompt casualties among unprotected troops; to force the other side into a cumbersome protective posture that reduces force effectiveness; or to deny access to, or easy use of, key facilities such as airfields, ports, supply depots, or command centers. With chemical weapons, the user has some ability to tailor effects to meet various tactical requirements. For example, if a field commander faces opposing forces at close range, he might choose a "nonpersistent" chemical, such as the nerve agents GB or GD, which would dissipate after several minutes or hours, allowing his forces to retake territory with minimal threat of exposure. Correspondingly, for targets farther behind the front lines, the commander might employ a "persistent" agent, such as mustard or the nerve agent VX, to bog down operations at, say, an airbase for a period of days or weeks.

Chemicals are not without their drawbacks, however. Chemical attacks are inherently sensitive to the topographical characteristics of the target area and to local weather conditions—barometric pressure, wind patterns, precipitation—that are beyond the control of local commanders. For these reasons, the effectiveness of chemical attacks will always be hard to predict. Another problem is downwind drift. Depending on the size of an attack and the wind velocity, military planners must prudently assume a downwind hazard—not only to civilians and enemy troops, but also to friendly forces—of potentially tens of kilometers in range. Finally, there is the issue of defensive responses to CW. The toxic effect of all known chemical agents can be greatly reduced or defeated for periods of time with the expeditious use of CW protective measures. Beyond a rate of fire that forces the other side to "suit up" with defense gear, additional CW munitions are less effective than the lethal effect of a corresponding inventory of high explosive (HE) munitions.

Generally, defensive measures fall into two categories: individual and collective protection. Individual measures encompass the gas mask, overgarments, gloves, boots, and other gear designed to enable troops to fight in a chemically contaminated environment. Collective measures include things such as air-filtration systems in motor vehicles or protective shelters at command centers and airbases that provide a clean environment for combat and support personnel. Naturally, any defensive posture also requires alarms or detection systems to reliably alert personnel to the presence of toxic chemicals, as well as procedures to avoid contamination or to decontaminate land vehicles, aircraft, ships, supplies, and personnel in protective gear. Finally, adequate training and exercising of troops is critical to the effectiveness of one's overall defensive posture.

While defensive measures are numerous, many of them impose some penalty on combat efficiency. Indeed the value of chemical weapons is often calculated more in terms of their ability to force the other side into a defensive posture than in their direct impact on combat casualties. For example, some commanders estimate these defensive means may cut the effectiveness of their combat units in half in some situations. Protective gear is typically bulky and uncomfortable. It cuts down on maneuverability, vision, and communication with comrades and commanders. Heat exhaustion may become a severe problem, depending on local weather conditions. Collective measures have other drawbacks. They are inherently constraining—flight crews cannot easily service aircraft if confined to shelters—and there is always the risk of inadvertent contamination with personnel frequently moving in and out of protected areas. Decontamination is a time-consuming, labor intensive, and risky operation. In coping with a chemical threat, field commanders would have to face hard trade-offs between ensuring protection of troops against CW attacks and maintaining the performance of the military unit as a whole. CW is only one of the many threats encountered on the battlefield. While the desire for maximum protection is natural, it may be self-defeating. Some heightened exposure to risk may be necessary to preserve one's overall position in conventional military operations.

## The Impact of New Technologies

What of the impact of new technologies?[5] Developments now underway could, in principle, augment CW capabilities substantially. On the offensive side, the major focus is on more prompt, accurate delivery systems, such as tactical missiles, and on dispersal techniques that make it easier to reproduce the "footprint" of a chemical weapon's toxic effects under a variety of environmental conditions. (However, even precise delivery does not substantially negate the problem of chemicals drifting away from target areas and into civilian areas.) Other technologies will make CW easier to handle. The new "binary" chemical artillery shells and bombs that the United States has in development are not essentially more lethal than the munitions they will replace (indeed, they may be less so); but they would be safer to store, service, and transport since, as their name implies, their constituent chemical compounds are not lethally toxic until mixed together just prior to the weapon's arrival over the target.[6]

On the defensive side, new technologies will help to improve the quality of protective gear and spur the further development of new, more reliable detection and alarm systems. With better intelligence and communications systems, field commanders and their troops should be able to prosecute combat operations at lower levels of CW defensive readiness with far less risk of being caught off guard. At the same time, no fundamentally new defensive concepts are in prospect. Major breakthroughs on antidotes or other ways to neutralize chemical attacks are highly unlikely. What looks more achievable is an extrapolation of present trends toward more flexible decontamination techniques and less cumbrous protective clothing.

A special concern in this area is the possibility that new, more lethal forms of chemical or biological agents could be developed to defeat defensive measures. In theory, new biotechnologies will make it possible to produce genetically engineered toxins that are more diverse and many orders of magnitude more lethal than existing chemical agents. Yet, not enough is known to form conclusive judgments about their military potential. It is certainly possible that toxin agents, once developed, might proliferate to other countries fairly easily, giving their possessors something approaching a mass destruction capability against large populations. Unlike biological weapons, whose propensity to spread epidemics would be difficult to control, toxins have effects that are both noninfectious and rapid, making them potentially valuable as battlefield weapons. Moreover, detection of toxins on the battlefield might be problematic unless our intelligence is good enough to keep track of evolving threats and unless we translate that knowledge into reliable alarms and protective clothing.

At the same time, it is far from clear that toxins would be superior to nerve agents in tactical situations. The greater lethality of toxins would not necessarily translate into reduced weapons requirements since chemical weapons are already a small component of overall force posture, and the vast majority of the weight in these weapons is associated with the delivery systems, not the toxic substance. Beyond this, although defensive technologies will be hard pressed to keep pace with modernization on the offensive side, it seems improbable that technological changes per se would put the defense at a disadvantage in any decisive way, provided that Western intelligence is adequate to give warning of new and threatening developments.

## Warsaw Pact Capabilities

Given the attributes of the chemical battlefield discussed above, how important is the chemical option for the Soviet Union and its Warsaw Pact allies? The Soviet military traditionally has placed great emphasis on preparations for all aspects of chemical warfare. However, intelligence on the Soviets' motives and planning is sparse, and there is little in their current literature on operational doctrine to suggest that they stress the CW option.[7] Instead, the evidence regarding the Soviet chemical posture emerges with varying degrees of clarity from several sources.

First, the Soviets invest substantial amounts in protective measures. Western intelligence has developed a fairly detailed knowledge of Soviet NBC (nuclear/biological/chemical) defenses over the years. The Soviets outfit their forces with a full array of individual protective gear; they equip many of their standard transport and attack systems (e.g., tanks, self-propelled artillery, armored personnel carriers), support vehicles, and command posts with collective protection; and they maintain specially organized units that are responsible for NBC training, reconnaissance, and decontamination. While it would be misleading to say that these preparations are mainly focused on chemical (as opposed to radiological) effects, or that their prime purpose is to confer on Soviet forces the ability to initiate CW attacks without regard to the effects of Western retaliation, the scale of Soviet efforts is impressive. Soviet defensive programs exceed comparable efforts in the West, and some experts point out that Soviet investment in these programs occurred at a time when Western capabilities were declining.[8]

A second indicator of Soviet capability is its chemical weapons stockpile. Soviet stocks are thought to be quite diverse. Included are several classes of nerve agents, mustard and lewisite, hydrogen cyanide, phosgene, and incapacitants of an unspecified nature. According to the U.S. government, there is also evidence to suggest that the Soviets retain or may be developing biological weapons and toxin agents.[9] Unfortunately, intelligence on the size of Soviet stocks is very sketchy. Estimates range enormously, from 20,000 metric tons, which is somewhat below public estimates of the level of U.S. stocks, to vast quantities exceeding 500,000 to 700,000 tons.[10] It is also unclear how much of the Soviet stockpile is available for immediate use. The Soviets apparently store much of their stocks in bulk form. Nonetheless, the scale of known Soviet mustard and nerve gas production facilities seems incompatible with anything less than a major weapons program.

A third, notable feature of the Soviet posture is its range of CW-capable delivery systems. Here, the diversity of Soviet systems relative to the West is particularly striking. Reportedly, all Soviet heavy artillery systems, multiple rocket launch systems, as well as certain types of rotary and fixed wing aircraft have compatible CW shells, rock-

ets, and bombs.[11] Of special concern for NATO is the fact
that Soviet short-range ballistic missiles (SRBMs)—the SS-
21, SS-23, SS-22—are thought to have a CW capability.
The portion of these missiles assigned routinely to CW
attack missions is unknown. But some experts speculate
that the Soviets might use these systems to attack long-
range targets, such as airfields, ports, nuclear weapons
depots, and command sites in order to blunt a coherent
response to a Soviet conventional attack.

## What Kind of Threat Do Pact Capabilities Pose?

Overall, it seems unmistakable that the Soviets forces are
well trained and equipped to engage in chemical warfare.
Again, the key question for this analysis is: how likely is it
that they would resort to chemicals and with what in-
tended result? Sound judgments about Western deterrent
needs should be sensitive not only to estimates of the
other side's posture, but also to its operational significance
and to the situations in which Pact commanders might
have strong incentive to use their arsenal. It is one thing to
say that CW is one option among several to be used in
conventional attacks against NATO forces, but quite another to argue that CW is a decisive element in Soviet war
planning.

Questions surrounding the role of chemical weapons
feed into the broader issue of a growing emphasis on
conventional warfighting in Warsaw Pact strategy.[12] The
key issue is whether CW might assume a greater role in
Soviet planning in situations where the military command
chose to withhold nuclear weapons in order to avoid
triggering a Western nuclear response. In the past, it was
thought that Soviet forces would most probably attempt to
destroy NATO defenses by resorting to nuclear weapons
at the outset of any conflict. Now, there is a growing

consensus among Western experts that Soviet planning (and the direction of Soviet weapons procurement) places much higher importance on a nonnuclear, high speed offensive. Under such a scenario, Soviet and Warsaw Pact commanders would attack massively, on short warning, with conventional forces in order to degrade NATO's forward defenses and to cripple its air forces at the outset of conflict. Their aim would then be to achieve rapid breakthroughs and large territorial gains in the first few days of fighting—preempting NATO's option to escalate—without resort to nuclear weapons.

There is disagreement regarding the importance of CW to this concept of operations. Some observers believe that the Soviets see CW as a decisive substitute for nuclear weapons and as a counterweight to NATO's conventional force improvements. In the opening phases of conflict, Soviet forces would launch full-scale attacks on rear targets with aircraft and their short- and medium-range ballistic missiles. The improving accuracies of these missile systems, especially the SS-21, would permit some substitution of chemical for nuclear warheads while falling short of the super accuracies that would make conventional warheads a preferable substitute for either. Although this kind of "quasi-strategic" attack might be dangerous from the standpoint of escalating the conflict, some observers point out that it need not be massive, but could be limited in time and scale to selected targets. "Selective" attack would, in theory, make it harder for NATO to agree on a nuclear response.

Meanwhile, closer to the battlefront, Warsaw Pact forces would attempt to break through NATO's forward defenses along several axes of advance. Again, selective or massive localized CW attacks would lend strength to this effort. Such attacks would help to impair the build-up of NATO conventional defenses, disrupt their logistical base, or simply force Western troops to don their protective

gear, thereby slowing their ability to maneuver. According
to some analyses, integrated use of chemicals could deci-
sively accelerate the overall pace of the Warsaw Pact
offensive and contribute to the Soviet's basic strategic
objective of handing NATO a decisive "short war" defeat
before it has any chance to contemplate escalation.

Another, opposing viewpoint in the debate holds that
chemical weapons are not a central element in Warsaw
Pact planning, and that claims of heavy reliance on CW
are greatly exaggerated. Observers taking this position
generally argue that the trade-offs of using chemicals over
conventional HE munitions are potentially quite severe. In
purely tactical situations, for example, any employment of
chemicals large enough to saturate NATO's forward defenses might actually constrain the Pact's offensive by
hampering the ability of Pact commanders to sustain a
high rate of fire of HE shells. Moreover, it is argued that
the effects of chemical attacks would be far less predictable, hinging to a large extent on the vagaries of local
atmospheric conditions. For instance, any Soviet CW use
at close quarters would force Soviet troops to don protective gear simply to avoid contamination from the drifting
effects of their own weapons. In Central Europe, local
wind conditions vary, and weather systems often move in
an easterly direction. Thus, in some cases, Soviet use of
chemicals might actually slow down their blitzkrieg-style
attack. In any case, it would make any attack heavily
dependent on local weather conditions.

The same problem, say the skeptics, broadly applies to
most quasi-strategic uses of CW. Under selective-use scenarios, it is unclear how much confidence chemicals
would offer in terms of disrupting NATO's combat operations for a specified period of time. Clearly, any massive
use, these observers argue, would dramatically increase
the risks of triggering a nuclear response by NATO. In
general, even though most skeptics acknowledge the

Pact's capacity to engage in chemical attacks, they deny that CW is a vital part of their concept of operations.

These two schools of thought tend to mark the polar extremes of the debate. Both have obvious drawbacks. For example, those who see CW as pivotal in Soviet strategy often gloss over the basic incompatibility between chemicals and the high intensity, time-urgent conventional scenarios within which they would be employed. For conservative Soviet war planners, CW is not likely to be a preferred option in the execution of high-speed conventional attacks. With rapidly changing weather patterns that are common to Europe and the likelihood of protection on the other side, chemical weapons are unlikely to offer the benefits of precise employment or predictable effect, except against large and unprotected area targets. Pact commanders could not ignore the risk of retaliation, and, even if a response were limited, they could not discount the possibility that substantial downwind drift of their chemicals would bog down their forward advance in neighboring sectors.

Yet, the weakness of the skeptics' position is that it tends to neglect the potential benefits to the Pact of selective CW use aimed at exploiting advantages of surprise or lack of preparedness. The cost/benefit calculations that shape the incentives of Pact commanders are in no sense immutable; they depend heavily on NATO's own posture. Thus, although CW munitions may compare poorly relative to HE munitions in many attack scenarios, Warsaw Pact forces might well recalculate their plans in favor of CW if there were obvious deficiencies in NATO's defensive posture or if there were no risk of triggering retaliation in kind. More fundamentally, in certain selected scenarios like long-range attacks with ballistic missiles, the Pact may have *no other option* except CW if it wishes to avoid using nuclear weapons.[13] The Eastern bloc has not yet matched the West in terms of developing the

super accuracies for air or ballistic missile delivery systems
that would make HE munitions an attractive option for,
say, the airfield attack mission.

In assessing these opposing positions, two general observations seem germane:

> *First,* the idea that the Soviets view CW as a ready
> substitute for nuclear weapons seems improbable.
> Although the Pact might view chemicals as being
> more effective than conventional weapons against
> certain area targets and more "usable" than nuclear
> weapons, chemical weapons are still weapons of
> mass destruction, and their use in any decisive way,
> especially against distant targets, would raise pre-
> cisely the sorts of escalatory risks that the Pact would
> want to avoid.
>
> *Second,* the battlefield conditions favoring the CW
> option are so specialized as to argue against any *high
> degree* of reliance by the Pact on the initial use of
> chemicals to sustain a breakthrough. Pact com-
> manders may not have the luxury of waiting for a
> sunny day with light variable winds, when CW
> would be of optimal military value, to launch their
> campaign; they will want to be prepared to engage
> their forces under any circumstances.

These foregoing observations should not be taken to
mean that the Soviets or their Pact allies would forbear in
the use of chemicals if they saw some advantage in doing
so, but only that CW is probably not viewed by them as a
decisive asset in the calculation of whether to launch an
attack. Overall, CW does not appear to be a "weapon of
choice" for the Warsaw Pact. In measuring the characteristics of chemical arms against the Warsaw Pact's concept of
operations, the most plausible interpretation of its CW
planning is one that favors optional use on a selective
basis. Thus, Warsaw Pact forces might resort to CW if

their conventional campaign were faltering, if NATO presented attractive targets, if Pact commanders sensed no
risk of retaliation as a consequence of their own use of
CW, or if (in the unlikely event) the United States altered
its rules of engagement and used chemicals first. But CW
is probably not, in any sense, a priority option set apart
from these other considerations.

# 2

# NATO'S CAPABILITIES AND FUTURE OPTIONS

What paths are open to NATO in preserving deterrence of chemical use? As an abstract proposition, virtually everyone agrees on the importance of deterrence. NATO must do all that is prudently possible to dissuade the Warsaw Pact from the idea that it could gain a decisive edge by using chemical weapons. The problem lies in translating this general desire into concrete steps. Deterrence is an elusive concept. Because we cannot know precisely when or why it works, we can never be totally confident in how best to keep it robust. Naturally, this quality of uncertainty leads to controversy. The measures that one person may regard as being prudent and necessary may seem extreme and wasteful to another.

## NATO'S Present Posture

Any discussion of options must begin with NATO's current posture. In general, CW programs vary greatly throughout the alliance. Most of NATO's effort falls into the category of defensive measures. Britain, West Germany, France, the Netherlands, and several other allies have defensive CW programs—some of them more technically sophisticated than U.S. efforts, which flagged badly during the early 1970s. As a result of NATO's long-term defense program, initiated during the latter 1970s, there has been a marked improvement in the availability of state-of-the-art overgarments, masks, and other items of individual protection. The United States has also improved the quality of training and protection programs, expanded them to all the military services, and has increased the number of chemical specialists assigned to various units. For certain items, like overgarments, the standard of NATO equipment is thought to be superior to that of the Warsaw Pact side. This might give Western troops some advantage if both sides were forced to operate "suited up." But in other areas—notably collective protection for command centers, airbases, ships, and battlefield vehicles, as well as overall training and exercising of troops—the quality of programs in Western countries is very uneven.

As for its retaliatory requirements, NATO relies exclusively on the United States CW arsenal. Existing U.S. chemical weapons date back to the 1950s and 1960s. None have been produced since. U.S. inventories include both persistent (VX) and nonpersistent (GB) classes of nerve agent, mustard agent, and the incapacitant BZ. About 40 percent of current U.S. stocks are in the form of munitions, including artillery and howitzer shells, several types of bombs, spray tanks, mortars, and battlefield rockets. The remaining 60 percent or so is stored in bulk form, rather than in weapons. As noted earlier, the United States maintains a small stockpile of weapons (all artillery shells) in the Federal Republic. Most of the munitions and all of the bulk agent are stored in the United States.[14]

Considerable controversy has surrounded the status of existing U.S. stocks in recent years. Many say that the stockpile has aged badly and is no longer militarily effective. U.S. Department of Defense officials concluded in 1984 that only about 28 percent of the current inventory could be put to any military use at all. But this claim is disputed by others. A 1985 presidentially appointed panel, which came out in favor of the Administration's proposals for new binary weapons, termed the Pentagon's figures "unduly pessimistic."[15] The panel found no data to support the view that the potency of existing munitions had substantially declined. It also investigated charges of major safety problems arising from leaky or unstable munitions, and concluded that the allegations were greatly exaggerated and misleading. Meanwhile, the U.S. Army has announced plans to dispose of older stocks in the inventory, starting with those that pose hazards for continued storage in the near term.

Although the reliability of these munitions remains a matter of dispute, the operational limitations associated with the present stockpile are plainly severe. Many of the munitions are not appropriately matched to assigned missions. For example, a large portion of the artillery shells is filled with persistent agent while current tactics for short-range bombardment call only for nonpersistent effects (in part to reduce exposure to friendly forces). Correspondingly, all of the existing bombs are filled with nonpersistent agent, which the Pentagon argues would be of little value against longer range fixed targets. The stockpile also includes outdated or nonoperational delivery systems (e.g., spray tanks, battlefield rockets), and lacks any readily available means to convert bulk agents into munitions. Moreover, some military experts lay great stress on the lack of any long-range delivery capability. With current stocks in Europe, the United States could muster a limited retaliation at short ranges. But it does not possess—anywhere—the significant means to respond in kind to CW attacks on targets in rear areas.

## What Options Could NATO Pursue?

In principle, NATO could take three kinds of steps to augment its posture. It could invest in better defensive protection; it could pursue "non-CW" responses as a way to help deter chemical attacks; it could lend further support for maintaining or modernizing the U.S. stockpile of chemical weapons. The extent to which each of these steps—either singly or in combination—should be pursued and at what cost are difficult questions. Perceptions of deterrence differ and circumstances change. Even so, in thinking through NATO's options, we should keep in mind several basic considerations:

> *First,* the deterrent role played by NATO's CW posture is a highly specialized one. The alliance's preeminent concern with chemical deterrence is to influence the Warsaw Pact's choices about the conduct of war *once it has begun.* In peacetime or in situations short of war, the inhibitions affecting the Pact's more fundamental prior decision—whether to attack at all—are reinforced more fundamentally by the nuclear and conventional components of NATO's posture. CW may contribute to these inhibitions, but only incrementally.

> *Second,* within the confines of the wartime deterrence situation, Pact incentives to use chemicals are probably more sensitive to NATO's own CW posture than is commonly realized. Recall our earlier discussion of Pact options. If massive chemical attacks were really central to Pact planning, no form of deterrence—perhaps not even nuclear weapons—would likely induce its commanders to forbear once war broke out. Conversely, if chemicals were so impractical as to be of no military value, deterrence would not be necessary. The reality lies somewhere in between.

"Selective" use could be deterred if the Pact were convinced it could gain no enduring advantage by resort to chemical weapons.

*Third,* any choices regarding modernization of NATO's CW posture should be sensitive to the criterion of operational effectiveness. Because CW deterrence is calculated mainly as a function of its contribution to preserving NATO's position on the battlefield, special attention should be paid to the relative value of (and trade-offs between) CW and HE munitions in use against the same targets. Chemical weapons are not likely to enhance deterrence very much if the marginal costs of delivery are high and if chemical weapons are perceived to be displacing conventional weapons that could have more enduring destructive effects.

What do these general considerations suggest for NATO's CW policies?[16] To start with, they underscore the importance of augmenting NATO's defensive posture. Defensive measures enhance NATO's fighting flexibility and therefore contribute to the specialized form of deterrence at stake with chemical warfare. Indeed, defensive measures provide an aspect of deterrence that the threat of retaliation cannot match: if Pact commanders did not have to contend with NATO defenses, they might well conclude that triggering response in kind would be a small price to pay for the option of devastating unprotected Western forces with chemical attacks. However, provided defenses are adequate, such "cheap shots" are not a real prospect. Pact commanders cannot be sure of being able to degrade NATO's forces beyond the level that protection itself imposes on the defending force. This fact alone might drive up the costs of CW attack options to thresholds that would risk cutting into the Pact's conventional posture or triggering a nuclear response. Defensive measures also complement NATO's other passive forms of defense against conventional or nuclear attack.

NATO's investments in CW defenses should be targeted to specific needs. Greater research into the dynamics of combat operations in a chemical environment could improve knowledge about the nature of combat degradation imposed by protective gear, and thus help to inform choices on new designs for overgarments, masks, and other items. More compact CW alarm systems are being developed to provide better, more reliable detection of a larger range of agents, to identify the type of agent being used, and to give an "all-clear" signal so that troops could dispense with protection more rapidly. Better collective protection—to enable personnel at command posts and airbases to function effectively under hazardous conditions—should receive a much higher priority as should innovative decontamination techniques that neutralize the toxic effluent resulting from the "washing down" of equipment. Finally, and very importantly, more extensive and better coordinated training programs would enable NATO to achieve a higher, more uniform standard of protection throughout the alliance.

In augmenting CW protection, emphasis should be given to those systems and technologies that enable forces to respond flexibly to changing levels of threat. As noted earlier, the natural tendency on the battlefield is to assure protection at levels that may not be optimal in terms of combat efficiency. While adequate protection is critical, too much of it can be self-defeating. NATO's overall approach to defensive measures should therefore be selective. The alliance does not need to develop a major new defense initiative, but rather to accelerate some of the improvements already set in motion.

In key areas, "non-CW" initiatives might also contribute to the overall robustness of NATO's CW defenses. For instance, improved tactical communications would give

local NATO commanders better knowledge of whether
CW had been used in adjoining sectors, and thus provide
a stronger information base to make decisions on defensive readiness. In addition, new air defense weapons,
conventional mid-range interdiction capabilities, and (potentially) anti-tactical ballistic missiles (ATBMs) could discourage Soviet efforts to engage in deep strike attacks.
Non-CW initiatives are distinct from other measures in
that they contribute more directly to NATO conventional
capabilities. For precisely that reason, however, they must
be justified in large part on the basis of needs outside the
CW arena. Their contribution to CW deterrence is difficult
to distinguish from their broader role in NATO's overall
conventional defense.

This brings us to the retaliatory component of the CW
posture. What kind of role does it play? As previously
suggested, since inadequate protection would run the
ever-present risk of "cheap shot" attacks, defensive
measures provide a certain type of deterrence to first use
that a retaliatory posture cannot match. Furthermore,
nuclear weapons unavoidably play a role in deterrence. If
the Soviet use of CW were seen as a pivotal factor in
turning the tide of battle against NATO, Western leaders
would have to face up to the question of deliberate escalation in any case. Yet, it is doubtful that nuclear weapons
provide a credible form of wartime deterrence to less than
massive, quasi-strategic attacks. To assert reliance on nuclear deterrence for this contingency would be inconsis-
tent with NATO's expressed desire to avoid the early use
of nuclear weapons by augmenting its nonnuclear posture. Nor would more defensive or non-CW initiatives
alone be sufficient for deterrence. Even with a greatly
enhanced defensive posture, the Pact could still gain a
very important battlefield advantage by prosecuting a CW
attack with impunity—that is, by forcing NATO troops to
"suit up" without having to do so itself. Denying that

option to the Pact is a critical factor in chemical deterrence, one that justifies possession of CW weapons in the absence of major new agreements to reliably ban them on both sides.

## The Production of New Weapons

If deterrence of chemical attacks requires some capacity to retaliate in kind, does it follow that new weapons are required to meet this goal? And, if so, are binary systems desirable? In recent years, these questions have proved difficult to sort out. Defense measures, after all, have a certain self-evident virtue. Who can be against defense? By contrast, offense—if only to threaten retaliation—is inherently more controversial. At the heart of this debate is the current U.S. program to acquire binary weapons: a 155 mm. artillery shell, for use at short ranges; a glide bomb, called the *Bigeye*, which would be delivered by fighter bombers against Pact airbases and other fixed targets in rear areas; and, eventually, a multiple rocket launch system (MRLS) that would target opposing forces at intermediate ranges of 30–40 kilometers. The total acquisition cost of the artillery shell and the *Bigeye* is estimated to be about $2 billion. This amount roughly equals the cost of disposing of the much larger amount of existing stock that the new weapons would replace.

The modernization issue brings into sharp focus conflicting views of deterrence needs. Proponents believe that new weapons are needed to fill critical gaps in NATO's deterrent posture left open by the shortcomings of the existing stockpile. They stress in particular the operational flexibility of binary weapons. Because their ingredients are not lethally toxic prior to use, binary weapons are intrinsically safer to handle, more transportable, and more survivable (i.e., difficult for the other side to target). For example, the storage of binaries need not be confined to highly centralized facilities; they could be deployed in areas where the peacetime storage of existing chemicals is disallowed, such as on ships and at airbases. Moreover, proponents argue that new binary weapons would provide NATO with the capability to retaliate effectively throughout the depth of the theater of operations, using artillery shells with nonpersistent agent on short-range battlefield targets and the *Bigeye* with persistent agent against more distant targets. In general, proponents of modernization tend to place a high deterrent value on being able to retaliate to the Pact's first use at the level it occurs.

Opponents differ sharply in their net assessment of the costs and benefits of new weapons. By and large, they view the contribution of new munitions as being marginal at best to the deterrence of CW use that already exists. Most opponents do not see the limitations of the existing stocks as a serious obstacle to an adequate chemical deterrent. They point out that there are sufficient numbers of artillery shells available for short-range response. Conversely, the idea of developing a long-range CW attack option seems unimportant to the opponents. Many single out *Bigeye* for special criticism. Critics say it is not a cost-effective way to attack targets like airfields; that the technologies for delivering binary weapons at long ranges are not sufficiently developed; and that *Bigeye's* technique for dispersing chemical agent renders high-value delivery systems (i.e. aircraft) vulnerable to ground fire and poses a disproportionate risk to civilians.[17] Finally, the greater flexibility of binary weapons is purchased at considerable cost in operational terms, according to some critics. Because these weapons are technically complex (especially the *Bigeye*) and will never be tested to the extent that existing munitions have been, they must be judged as less reliable.

## Are Peacetime Deployments in Europe Necessary?

The debate over weapons would be difficult enough to resolve if binaries were the only issue. Recently, the question of *where* chemical weapons should be based has begun to receive prominent attention. As noted earlier, the United States has agreed to withdraw its existing CW stocks from the Federal Republic in return for NATO's endorsement of a "force goal" calling for implementation of the binary program. This arrangement, worked out by President Reagan and Chancellor Helmut Kohl and endorsed by NATO's Defense Planning Committee in May 1986, adds a new dimension to the modernization issue. In principle, the United States could retain existing stocks in Europe at the expense of building new ones, or it could replace existing systems with binary weapons for deployment with U.S. forces outside of Europe. But it could not produce new weapons *and* station them in Europe, at least in peacetime.

Clearly, the F.R.G.—U.S. understanding was designed to accomplish certain immediate objectives. On one hand, it enabled the Reagan Administration to obtain an important measure of support within NATO for its CW plans, which many in the Congress see as a prerequisite for the funding of binary weapons. On the other hand, the arrangement promises to shelter the West German government from a difficult and growing public debate over existing weapons and a potential dispute over whether to accept new U.S. weapons, especially when other key allies—including Britain and Italy—have already said they would not accept them in peacetime. In a sense, then, alliance solidarity has been well served by avoiding a neutron bomb-like debate over chemicals. The key question is: what are the consequences of this arrangement for security?

A number of experts have questioned the F.R.G.—U.S.

understanding on deterrence grounds. They contend that the pre-positioned munitions in West Germany would be a critical factor inhibiting Soviet first-use on the battlefield in the opening days of an attack, and that getting permission for an emergency redeployment of chemical weapons in time to reinforce deterrence is highly improbable. Interestingly, those counting themselves as skeptics on this issue include not only supporters of the binary program, who believe that forward basing is preferable to any other arrangement, but also some key opponents, who have maintained that existing stocks were always enough of a deterrent. Both tend to stress that emergency redeployment would be seen as provocative—potentially deepening a crisis situation—and that once war broke out, chemical weapons shipments would displace (or be displaced by) other critical reinforcements. As it is, U.S. airlift requirements, they point out, already greatly exceed available capacity. For fiscal year 1987, the Pentagon projects a global airlift goal of 66.7 million ton miles per day (amounting to over 611 sorties of C-141 payload equivalents) for rapid reinforcement of U.S. forces overseas. Available capacity is only about 60 percent of this figure, however, leaving a shortfall of about 25 million ton miles (or 232 sorties) that would cut heavily into major airlift requirements, especially to Europe.[18] Shipment by sea is always possible but would delay arrival by several weeks.

Other experts, while acknowledging the risks of emergency redeployment, insist that binary weapons would still be preferable to existing stocks despite the loss of peacetime deployment in Europe. Even the "worst case" Pact offensive, they say, would require mobilization of several days to a week or more, and this would provide some warning time. In such circumstances, binary munitions, especially bombs, would be much easier to transport quickly. Provided that advance planning were done properly, the United States could shift a limited supply of CW stocks to Europe within a few days—maybe even more quickly (and certainly more safely) than dispersing existing unitary munitions from their single, vulnerable storage location in West Germany. Moreover, these experts say, one should be careful not to focus too narrowly on the unique difficulties of obtaining permission for the redeployment of chemicals. Adverse domestic reactions might well be a less decisive factor in government decision-making in a crisis than in peacetime. In any case, European leaders would have to make many other decisions on generating reinforcements and reserves in the face of Pact preparations for war. Thus, to some extent, binary shipments might be "lost in the noise" of a general mobilization.

Of course, it is very difficult to say which one of these viewpoints would obtain in the buildup to a major conflict. Much would depend on the circumstances of the moment, and some deterrent effect would exist despite the uncertainty. However, the case for new, more transportable munitions becomes much stronger if one postulates a world in which there is no more peacetime deployment in Europe, and rapid deployment of weapons (given adequate air lift) becomes more critical to preserving a retaliatory option.

## Sizing Up the Alternatives

The foregoing discussion of NATO's capabilities and options points to a number of important conclusions. First, as a general approach to maintaining chemical deterrence, NATO needs a mix of initiatives. Defensive measures, non-CW responses, and new weapons are unlikely to be sufficient if pursued individually. At the same time, the proper "mix" is one that highlights defense over offense. NATO does not need a chemical warfighting capability. Nor does it need to match the Warsaw Pact's chemical capability; there is no less deterrence for failing to do so.

What NATO needs is a relatively small stockpile—no more than a small fraction of the HE requirements—that could plausibly force the Pact into a defensive posture if it chose to use CW first. Anything more substantial might actually cut into NATO's ability to fight effectively with conventional weapons. In addition, it might be seen by the Soviets as evidence that NATO was attempting to substitute chemical for nuclear deterrence. That would have the perverse impact of reducing the deterrent value of NATO's posture overall and must be avoided.

A second and more debatable proposition is whether a modest CW retaliatory capability should include a capacity to strike distant targets. In deterrence terms, some long-range capability is probably desirable. Some military experts in the Federal Republic and the United States stress the priority of acquiring a long-range deterrent capability over short-range modernization; the idea of retaliating with short-range weapons to the other side's long-range attacks may not be very credible if the Pact has avoided using chemicals on the battlefield. At the same time, NATO has a decisive edge in developing high accuracy conventional delivery systems for long-range strikes against fixed targets. In strictly operational terms, the West may be better off using HE munitions, not chemicals. Moreover, the United States' only currently planned system for this mission—the *Bigeye* weapon—has problems. The bomb's design is based on 1960s vintage technology, and it has compiled an unsatisfactory record in development. Its agent, VX, may not prove very effective in slowing down operations at airbases given expected levels of protection on the other side. If so, it would not seem to meet the criterion of operational effectiveness that is important to wartime deterrence. Beyond this, concerns about its employment mode, reliability, and potential for indiscriminate damage to civilians, noted above, are further grounds for caution. In the next few years, a better alternative would be to develop a highly accurate "stand

off" weapon, perhaps using advanced cruise missle technology (if such proves feasible) to fulfill this particular
mission requirement if it is deemed necessary in operational terms.

Finally, there remains the issue of peacetime basing. On
deterrence grounds, the arguments in favor of having
some CW weapons available in Europe are clear. Reintro-
ducing these weapons to forward areas in a crisis is a
serious question. We simply cannot know in advance how
a military confrontation in Europe would unfold and how
political leaders on both sides of the Atlantic would react
under the growing stress generated by large-scale mobilization. On the other hand, a prudent Soviet planner could
not be sure that U.S. weapons would not be reintroduced
during the mobilization period. Moreover, even if the
F.R.G—U.S. understanding may not have been the best
choice, it has created a new political reality. Public expec-
tations of early withdrawal of these weapons have been
raised in West Germany. Perhaps the greatest danger is
that the bargain may excite criticism in Congress that the
allies are not doing enough to shoulder the burden of
basing. The risk is that some in Congress might attempt to
force the issue by holding any future modernization hos-
tage to an alliance agreement on peacetime deployment. If
so, we might end up with no modernization and no
basing in Europe and a huge alliance controversy over an
essentially secondary issue.

To exaggerate the dangers of the present situation
would, in fact, be a grave mistake. Emergency redeployment might not be more difficult than achieving timely
dispersal of European-based munitions to less vulnerable
locations. In addition, we may be able to expand our range
of options. NATO should investigate the possibility of pre-
positioning a portion of its stocks on ships in maritime
areas around Europe, or deploying a "quick reaction"
capability based around dedicated airlift or stand off missiles. (In either of these cases, binary technology would be

an important attribute of new systems, if only for its
contribution to safety and storage requirements.) These
alternatives might prove valuable in deterrence terms,
especially if they provided a more secure basis of public
support for alliance policies in this area.

# 3

# CW ARMS CONTROL: IS
# PROGRESS POSSIBLE?

The idea of restricting or banning chemical weapons has existed in one form or another since before the First World War. Talks involving the United States, the Soviet Union, key allies, and other countries have centered on a total ban in recent years. In one sense, a comprehensive ban involving large stocks of weapons—unprecedented as it is— seems too unreal to be taken seriously. But one need not hypothesize utopia to see the practical virtues of such a step. As noted above, chemical weapons are not held in high esteem within the Western alliance. Their capacity to inflict large-scale damage to civilian populations is a sensitive strategic and ethical issue. Political leaders are loath to justify their possession; military leaders would prefer not to have to fight with them. NATO would be better off if it could dispense with the burdens of chemical deterrence.

Unfortunately, the obstacles to success at the bargaining table are considerable. To start with, CW negotiations are extremely complex technically. Unlike nuclear weapons, chemical munitions are not very distinctive. They are not easy to count or to characterize with our technical means of verification. Their delivery systems are very diverse, and they share these systems with conventional forces. More generally, the industrial capacity to produce lethal chemical agents is widely distributed throughout the economies of all industrial countries. Most precursors of chemical weapons agents have legitimate uses in the civilian sector such as fertilizers and pesticides. This overlap makes durable and verifiable controls on CW conceptually hard to define, let alone negotiate. The political aspects of the CW problem are equally daunting. Soviet-American exchanges on CW are being conducted against a background of suspicions that the Soviets have violated existing agreements.[19] This adds to the burden of any new agreement the job of resolving outstanding grievances. Moreover, CW is inherently a multilateral issue. Because so many countries either possess chemical weapons or have the capacity to produce them, the simple model of bilateral superpower arms control is only a partial solution. Even if Moscow and Washington could work out a consensus approach to CW controls, they cannot assume that broad multilateral support would follow automatically, especially if key third world countries felt they were being handed a fait accompli by the superpowers.

These obstacles do not necessarily mean that useful agreements are beyond reach. Extensive controls or bans on CW are in fact an "option" that should be taken seriously precisely because chemical weapons are far less important than nuclear weapons to the stability of the East-West balance. The challenge of CW negotiations is to come up with a balanced diplomatic strategy that promises practical results in the near term but does not sacrifice the goal of a more comprehensive solution.

## The Existing Regime

The foundation of the present regime is the 1925 Geneva Protocol, which bans inter alia the "use in war of asphyxiating, poisonous or other gases. . . ." The Protocol, which is now generally (though not universally) recognized as codifying customary international law, has the character of a "no-first-use" pledge. Although the ban on use is not qualified within the Protocol itself, and is therefore binding on states even if they have been subjected to CW attacks, a number of key signatories—the United States, the Soviet Union, Britain, and France—expressly retain the right of retaliation in kind.[20] In 1972, the Protocol was supplemented by a multilateral ban on biological weapons. The BW Convention prohibits ". . . biological agents, or toxins . . . in quantities that have no justification for prophylactic, protective, or other peaceful purposes." An agreement strictly on BW had not been expected as the next step; it was long assumed that chemical and biological weapons would be dealt with under a comprehensive ban. But the key actors at the time felt that BW would be easier to restrict than chemicals and split the two issues into separate categories. Finally, in 1977, agreement was reached on the Environmental Modification Convention (ENMOD) that includes new constraints on herbicide warfare.[21]

This general regime is eroding under the stresses of a growing accumulation of problems. A basic shortcoming is, of course, its limited scope. Non-use agreements like the Geneva Protocol simply are not very constraining on countries that possess chemical weapons and that have some incentive to use them. As the number of countries armed with chemical weapons increases, CW threatens to become a potential source of instability in major regional rivalries, such as in the Korean peninsula, Southwest Asia (Iran, Iraq), and the Middle East (Syria, Israel, and Egypt). Beyond the question of scope, compliance standards in key provisions are not well defined. The Geneva Protocol is silent on how allegations of violations would be investigated. In the BW Convention, the issue of permitted levels of biological agent is not clearly spelled out. Nor is the BW Convention verifiable in the sense of being able to assess Soviet claims of compliance with any degree of confidence. (Biological weapons were widely viewed as having so little military value that no real verification was necessary.)

## Negotiations on a Comprehensive Ban

A comprehensive ban on CW has been widely heralded as the best way to strengthen the present partial regime. In 1977, the United States and the Soviet Union began bilateral discussions on banning CW. These talks stalled in 1979–80, ostensibly over verification issues, and broke off shortly thereafter. After a slow start in the early 1980s, the pace of diplomatic activity in the 40-nation Conference on Disarmament (CD) in Geneva picked up by 1983. The Soviet side showed increased flexibility on certain verification issues and tabled a major draft initiative in 1983. In 1984, the United States tabled a draft convention on CW and called for a resumption of bilateral "contacts" (as distinct from formal negotiations) aimed at resolving issues in the multilateral negotiations. Then, at the 1985 Geneva summit, President Reagan and Secretary Gorbachev affirmed their joint commitment to "accelerated" negotiations on CW leading to a total ban.

The course of CW diplomacy has been painstaking.[22] There is broad multilateral agreement on the types of chemicals to be covered within the scope of a ban and that the prohibition would include the development, production, stockpiling, transfer, and use of chemical weapons. There is also acceptance of the idea that existing CW stockpiles and production facilities would be declared promptly and destroyed within a period of 10 years. In addition, both sides have come closer to agreement in principle on key points regarding verification. The Soviets now accept the idea that the destruction of stockpiles and production means would be monitored continuously by an on-site inspection (OSI) procedure, and they seem to be moving toward acceptance of a quota for OSIs to verify the non-diversion of civil production facilities to military uses.

On other issues, however, the two sides remain at odds. They disagree fundamentally over the proper role of "challenge" OSIs (i.e., inspections requested by one side to investigate suspicious activity). In a hardening of previous positions, the United States now insists on a short-notice (48 hour) mandatory challenge inspection procedure that would allow U.S., Soviet, or other inspectors to check into possible noncompliance anywhere on national territory. To date, the Soviets have rejected anything more substantial than voluntary challenge inspections.[23] Further, while the Soviets are willing to declare the composition of their stocks, they have major reservations about the legitimacy of routine monitoring of stocks prior to destruction and are not willing to disclose the location of their stocks. Western countries take the view that declarations must include both composition and location data on stocks to assure an adequate baseline for compliance assessment.

In surveying the range of these disagreements, it is fair to ask how much more progress can reasonably be expected in the near term. The problems associated with reliable detection of undeclared stocks and production would be extremely difficult to resolve, even with unprecedented access to national territories. This is not to say that a total ban with some verification uncertainty might not achieve desirable goals. Some uncertainty might be deemed a fair price to pay for halting open-ended modernization, for beginning destruction of stocks, and for gaining the cooperation of the Soviet government on various forms of OSI. In addition, the security goal of denying the Soviets a well-honed offensive CW strike capability could probably be achieved without high confidence verification of all parts of a ban. Such a capability would require extensive testing and exercising and would be much harder to conceal than violations of the storage and production aspects of a prohibition.

Nonetheless, verification uncertainties cannot be lightly dismissed. It is inherently difficult to ascribe military significance to potentially undetectable violations. Even small-scale violations might increase in importance if there were reductions in conventional forces or if the existence of a treaty led the West to let up on its defensive measures against chemical weapons. Uncertainties are also politically risky. As we have seen with the BW Convention, provisions that cannot be verified with some degree of confidence leave open the risk of undermining the whole treaty if allegations of violations arise—even ones without any military significance—that cannot be disproved. Indeed, any treaties containing significant ambiguities would not be terribly resilient to future downturns in Soviet-American relations.

## Alternative Arms Control Approaches to CW

Are there more promising near-term paths to progress? Three types of regimes are often mentioned as alternatives to a comprehensive prohibition on chemical weapons: a chemical equivalent of the Nonproliferation Treaty (NPT); a nonzero limit that provides for retention of small CW stocks; and a regional CW "free zone." Each of these focuses on a rather different part of the problem.

*CW Nonproliferation.* Under the terms of a CW NPT, member states not possessing CW would formally renounce any intention to do so, and transfers of weapons between "have" and "have not" countries would be banned. Although the idea is not new, it gained prominence when Secretary Gorbachev announced after a summit meeting with French President Mitterand that the Soviet Union would be prepared to negotiate such an agreement. Subsequent news of informal Soviet-American talks on the subject led some to speculate that a bilateral initiative would be forthcoming at the Reagan-Gorbachev summit. However, the final communiqué spoke only of initiating "a dialogue on preventing the proliferation of chemical weapons."[24]

Clearly, one attraction of a CW NPT is that it represents the sort of diplomatic initiative on which the Soviet Union and the United States could cooperate. It would also deal with one of the most important current threats to the present non-use regime. Although an NPT-like restraint would not halt determined countries from acquiring CW, it would add much needed reinforcement to the idea that CW is not a type of military capability that states acquire as a matter of routine. Countries wishing to acquire CW legally—and hence refusing to join an NPT—would thus be forced into the uncomfortable position of drawing unwanted attention to themselves. However, on the negative side, unless it were accompanied by reduction or elimination of U.S. and Soviet stockpiles, an NPT for chemicals would antagonize much of the rest of the world. Many would see the idea as a tactic by the superpowers to sustain their own preeminence in the field. A number of countries with no current interest in acquiring CW weapons would refuse to join. This would tend to remove the onus from those who would refrain from joining because they wish to retain the CW option. In addition, an NPT would tend to confer unwarranted legitimacy on some countries—like North Korea and Syria—that already possess CW. Finally, it is not clear how early warning of potential violations could be readily achieved without extensive on-site safeguards analogous to those on the nuclear side provided by the International Atomic Energy Agency (IAEA).

*Nonzero Limitations.* The approach of negotiating stockpile cuts but not elimination of CW has been suggested as a way around some of the risks posed by a total ban.

Under such an agreement, parties would declare and
commence destruction of stocks and most production sites
within a specified period. But they would retain the right
to withhold small amounts for deterrence of violations by
adversaries. They would also undertake obligations not to
transfer or develop new weapons. The benefits of such a
step are readily apparent when one considers the current
suspicions that plague Soviet-American relations. Verification is widely and wrongly seen as an end in itself. It is
hard to imagine that any U.S. administration—even the
Reagan Administration—would be able to defend before a
skeptical Congress a treaty whose verification is problematic in key areas. But monitoring uncertainties would be
far easier to accept if small stocks were available under the
treaty as a hedge against violations. A total ban need not
be ruled out as a long-term goal.

Standing in the way of this approach, however, are
several complications. One has to do with multilateral
effects. An agreement that provides for anything less than
a total ban still, in effect, means some chemical weapons
for a few and no chemical weapons for many; it would be
the functional equivalent of a CW NPT treaty and would
share many of the liabilities of that approach. Another has
to do with the verification problems unique to limitations.
Under a ban, *any* evidence of stock retention or production would be grounds for suspecting a violation. Under a
limitation, the verifying party would face the harder task
of measuring the evidence obtained against the threshold
of permitted numbers or activities specified in an agreement. Even specifying "how much is enough" for finite
deterrence may be difficult to do conceptually. Thus, the
political reassurance to be gained by retaining some stocks
as a hedge may come at the cost of actually making the
verification problem harder, not easier.

*A CW "Free Zone."* Much attention recently has been
focused on the suggestion that the chemical arms of the
United States and the Soviet Union might be withdrawn

from parts or all of Europe, creating a CW "free zone."[25] In March 1984, delegations representing the West German Social Democratic Party (SPD) and East German Socialist Unity Party (SED) completed a draft initiative for such a zone. Some proposals, like that of the Palme Commission in 1981, provide only for forward disengagement along a narrow corridor of 150 kilometers or so on each side. The SPD/SED initiative calls for coverage of both Germanies and Czechoslovakia at a minimum, but also Poland, Belgium, Luxemburg, and the Netherlands. Whatever its geographical scope, the zone would provide for a ban on the stationing and production of chemical weapons and ban states from allowing transfer or transit of chemical weapons into or through national territories. Conceivably, the zone might be coupled to other negotiated steps involving the reduction or removal of nuclear weapons or conventional forces.

Proponents of the free zone idea often portray it as a helpful interim step on the road to a total ban. Negotiations leading to the removal of stocks, they say, would be an important confidence building measure and possibly stimulate progress in other areas of arms control. More recently, in the wake of the F.R.G.—U.S. decision to remove American CW stocks by the early 1990s, some skeptics have taken a more positive view of the zone. Since the West is committed to removing forward developments, the argument goes, why not obtain a withdrawal on the Warsaw Pact side in return? The resulting situation—a mutual withdrawal—would be better from the military standpoint than the F.R.G.—U.S. agreement which is essentially a unilateral, one-sided free zone.

Criticisms of the free zone idea have been advanced along several lines, however. First, many West Germans are loath to have the Federal Republic singled out for special status arrangements that have the effect of making their country a "no man's land" between East and West. They also object to legal restrictions that would tend to

concentrate weapons in westerly regions of their country
that are also the most industrialized and heavily popu-
lated. Current and former West German governments
have strongly opposed the zone idea for these reasons
alone. In addition, some observers doubt that a legally
binding zone would in fact be preferable to a situation of
one-sided withdrawal. Without a zone, the decision to
redeploy chemicals in a crisis would be NATO's own; the
Soviets could not exert a *droit de regard*. However, once a
zone were in place, any move by the Soviets to covertly
position their stocks in forward areas (and geographical
proximity gives them a clear advantage to do so) could not
be countered without embroiling the alliance in a huge
debate over treaty compliance. Finally, the verification of
such a zone is likely to prove difficult in practice. Non-
transfer of chemical weapons is among the hardest types
of activity to detect, and yet it would be crucial to the
integrity of the arrangement. Some experts point out that
all of the verification problems that now stand in the way
of a total ban would have to be solved before a free zone
could be implemented effectively.

## A Net Assessment

Comparing the pros and cons of these approaches relative
to a total ban is a difficult task. Much depends on highly
subjective judgments regarding the plausibility of
disarmament in its most ambitious form, and whether the
partial steps discussed above would contribute to or de-
tract from current negotiations. Many observers fear that
anything less than a total ban will eventually open the
way for the major powers to modernize their arsenals and
for other nations to develop arsenals, granting CW a
greater degree of legitimacy than it enjoys today. Besides,
they argue, no other goal in the area of disarmament has
gained such widespread support, ranging from the

Reagan Administration to most third world countries. Yet other observers cite the risks of the current strategy. The major problem, they say, is that if the international community holds out for a total ban, it may end up with nothing. Stalemate would only aggravate problems and suit those who oppose arms control in principle. In such circumstances, the best often becomes the enemy of the good.

Clearly, none of these partial measures can match a total, verifiable ban in terms of the range of constraining effects.[26] A CW free zone, for example, might have some confidence building effects, but with the prospect that the Soviets could reintroduce weapons quickly into Europe, it would be less resilient to breakout. Conversely, a nonzero CW agreement might offer some hedges to violations but would be harder to verify. More generally, a feature common to all CW proposals, including the total ban, is the obvious tension between gaining the initial objective of U.S. and Soviet consensus and then implementing the agreement effectively. For example, if the overriding goal were to maximize the prospect of Soviet-American cooperation, one would probably choose a nonzero limit on stocks or a CW NPT. But if the central goal were to secure broad multilateral adherence, neither of these approaches would be very popular. A CW free zone confined to Europe would avoid the necessity of having to gain broad multilateral adherence, but it might not prove negotiable since the Soviets need not offer anything in return for obtaining the presently scheduled withdrawal of U.S. stocks from the Federal Republic by the early 1990s.

What do these problems suggest for policy development? First, it might be worth seeking initiatives outside the realm of formal agreements in order to advance the goals of CW restraint. For example, a more productive way to deal with the proliferation of CW capabilities might be through a "suppliers group" approach. Such a group would not require adherence from recipient nations. In the wake of chemical weapons use in the Gulf War, several

Western governments imposed chemical export controls on trade with Iraq and Iran. The Soviet Union followed suit in January 1986 by attaching domestic restrictions on the sale of dual-use chemicals. Along with these individual actions there have been several diplomatic exchanges among supplier countries organized by the Australian government, including at least one Soviet-American meeting in Bern, Switzerland, that took place in 1986. Export restraint on the model of the "Nuclear Suppliers Group" would be harder to achieve in the CW area because the sources are so numerous, and many countries already have chemical infrastructure. Nevertheless, the pooling of intelligence resources on proliferation would help to broaden international awareness regarding countries attempting to acquire chemical weapons while avoiding the political problems surrounding a more formal NPT-like regime.

A second approach to CW arms control policy is to exploit overlaps between some of the partial steps and a total ban. For example, it need not be the case that a nonzero limitation on chemicals be portrayed as an alternative to a comprehensive agreement. The phased reduction of stocks over a period of years would itself provide, along with defense measures, the basis of finite deterrence to cheating. The parties could agree to review periodically their progress and the verification consequences of deeper cuts as they go along. With greater operational confidence in OSIs, they might choose to take the final step toward full disarmament. If not, they would have achieved at least an interim goal of substantial reduction and an important reassurance that such stocks as remain are well below the threshold needed to wage chemical attacks successfully.

# 4

# CONCLUSIONS

NATO faces a major challenge in devising effective policies for managing the chemical weapons issue. All the ingredients favoring a major controversy have fallen into place. Warsaw Pact chemical capabilities are an important issue for military planners, yet there are disagreements over what deterrence requires. The United States is embarking on a procurement program for new chemical weapons, but the basing of these and existing weapons is a potential source of tension. Banning CW is regarded as the best path to security, but opposing positions at the bargaining table do not augur well for progress.

If the answers to these problems were easy, there would be no controversy. Reasonable people may disagree over specific proposals. This report will succeed not by its promotion of specific proposals but if it helps to structure and clarify the debate over a sensitive issue in the allied democracies. Whatever one's conclusions on specific issues, certain basic points should be kept in mind.

1. *Chemical weaponry is a sensitive issue, but it is a second order issue compared to the importance of alliance unity in deterring a conventional or nuclear war in Europe.* Contro-

versy over modernization or deployment of chemical weapons should not be allowed to place political burdens on the alliance such as those that arose in the context of the neutron bomb or intermediate-range nuclear force (INF) decisions. The damage that disunity would do to deterrence would far outweigh the gains from optimal rather than less satisfactory military solutions to the deployment of chemical weaponry. For example, if the U.S. Executive Branch, Congress, and the NATO allies become involved in a tug of war over peacetime basing of chemicals in Europe, the result could be not only diminished chemical capabilities, but diminished deterrence overall.

2. *Given the importance of raising the nuclear threshold as well as deterring any war, few believe that NATO policy should allow nuclear deterrence to be the only means of deterring a chemical attack.* Nuclear deterrence is fundamental to preserving peace in Europe. However, in a wartime situation where the dividing line between war and peace had already been crossed, the idea of threatening nuclear retaliation to selective CW attacks may not be viewed as credible. To make such a threat credible would require an otherwise undesirable lowering of the nuclear threshold.

3. *The merits of the NATO decision to modernize chemical weapons while removing them from Europe in peacetime are highly debatable.* Clearly, the missing ingredient in NATO policy is an allied consensus that some chemical weapons have to be based in Europe in peacetime in order to deter Soviet CW use in the event of war. A U.S. chemical weapons presence in Europe is important politically and strategically. Without it, the United States increasingly becomes NATO's distant arsenal, whose capabilities are less likely to be effective in providing deterrence in a timely manner.

However, once the decision to remove chemical weapons has been made and publicized, it creates a new political reality. One should not pretend that sleeping dogs, once awakened, will return to somnolence. It is uncertain that it would be possible to retain chemical stockpiles in Germany, even if the recent NATO decision were reversed. Of course, one cannot rule out the possibility of a reversal; if it were possible, it would be desirable. Yet even if there is more deterrent value in chemical weapons that are forward based, it is not true that there is no deterrent value in weapons based outside of Europe. Prudent Soviet planners cannot count on the impossibility of chemical weapons being shipped to Europe during the mobilization period before a war begins. NATO now needs to devote attention to making sure such a capability exists.

4. *It is a mistake to exaggerate the Soviet chemical threat and to assume that NATO should have similar capabilities either in the quantity or type of stockpile.* The role of CW in NATO strategy is inherently limited. NATO needs enough chemical capability to ensure that there is symmetry in the degradation of NATO and Pact forces that results from "suiting up" with defensive measures. There is no operational or deterrent justification for NATO to acquire a large-scale chemical warfighting capability. As stated previously, nuclear weapons and conventional forces are much more fundamental to deterrence of aggression in Europe; it is short-sighted to think that chemical weapons would be a useful substitute for either. With a modest and mobile retaliatory force and a robust program of defensive measures, NATO's aim would be to deter selective use of CW and to ensure protection against chemical attacks with a minimum of disruption.

5. *The issue of binary weapon production has become an overly simple litmus test that draws attention away from other important questions.* While many, though not all, of those involved in this report believe that some modernization of the chemical stockpile is prudent, including modest numbers of one or two delivery systems of longer range, a number are skeptical about current plans for the acquisition of planned binary shells and bombs, for the reasons

given in Section 2. While some see the binary weapon as a conceptually sound means to achieve a smaller, safer stockpile, others doubt that the benefits of binary weapons outweigh their costs. But however one comes out on modernization issues, they should not draw attention away from the importance of continuing to develop more flexible and effective protective measures as an aspect of deterrence "by denial" in the chemical area.

6. *Chemical arms control should be accorded a higher priority in current negotiations, but one need not hold out for achievement of a total ban in order to obtain some progress.* For many years, Western leaders and publics have hoped that movement toward a CW ban would enable the alliance to avoid having to make hard choices about modernization and deterrence. Yet, as this analysis points out, the prospects for near-term breakthroughs are unlikely. Although much progress has been made, the remaining stumbling blocks are large and not easily overcome. Other arms control approaches sacrifice a degree of comprehensiveness but may offer greater payoff in terms of near-term progress. Some of their drawbacks may be alleviated if they are seen as steps toward an ultimate goal of a total ban. And coordination of intelligence and export controls among suppliers of chemicals should continue and be enhanced. Fortunately, the oft-cited contradiction between modernization and disarmament is not as sharp as is often made out. The process of modernization on the Western side could result in smaller stockpiles of weapons than exist today, while the United States' determination to acquire new weapons will arguably improve the Western negotiating posture.

It bears repeating that NATO would be far better off if both sides dispensed with chemical weapons in the long run. Only time will tell whether this judgment can be translated into widespread agreement on a durable ban. Soviet leaders may calculate that disarray within NATO on

CW would work to their interests. Current trends suggest that they may not need to negotiate an agreement to achieve substantial disarmament on the Western side. On the other hand, their assessment would be quite different if they reckoned that, in a wartime situation, their own first use of chemicals would force them to prepare for a chemical response or a substantial escalation of conflict. In that circumstance, they might well conclude that chemicals were not worth the costs and that the time had come to accelerate cooperation toward the ultimate goal of a total ban.

# ENDNOTES

1. Much of the sensitivity surrounding chemical weapons has been generated by public concerns over their potential wide area of lethal effects. For example, according to calculations by Professor Paul Doty of Harvard University, the employment of existing forward deployed U.S. stocks—publicly estimated at roughly 100,000 artillery shells—could create a lethal area on the order of 3,000 square kilometers. Given that the population density in West Germany averages about 200 persons per square kilometer, over 600,000 civilians would potentially be at risk from this level of use. The effects of a Soviet CW attack that would trigger a U.S. response might well double that estimate. While many experts point out that the use of CW might only be selective, and clearly not maximized to induce casualties among unprotected civilians, the sheer destructive potential of existing CW stocks and the threat of two-sided use attract significant concern.

2. France is the only other NATO ally thought to possess an appreciable CW capability, comprised mainly of short-range munitions. Recent reports indicate that France is preparing to produce new chemical weapons to ensure a capability to retaliate in kind. See J. Isnard, "Aggiornamento de la Doctrine," *Le Monde*, November 9/10, 1986. Although French forces—chemical and otherwise—are not integrated into NATO force structure, Warsaw Pact planners would have to take France's stockpile into account.

3. For further details on the proliferation problem, see Lois R. Ember, "Worldwide Spread of Chemical Arms Receiving Increased Attention," *Chemical and Engineering News*, April 14, 1986, pp. 8–16.

4. For a useful description of the types and properties of chemical warfare agents, see appendices in Edward M. Spiers, *Chemical Warfare* (Chicago: University of Illinois Press, 1986), pp. 208–213.

5. Parts of this section are based on presentation and discussion of analysis prepared by Dr. Paul Doty, Sir Ronald Mason, and Dr. Matthew Meselson at the Aspen/European Strategy Group workshop

on "Chemical Weapons and Western Security Policy," held at the Aspen Institute Berlin, June 12-14, 1986.

6. There is, however, a good deal of controversy over whether the safety advantages of binaries are outweighed by certain operational costs. Shipping components of binary weapons separately could tie up more airlift, and assembling the weapons under battlefield conditions could prove cumbersome and difficult.

7. Parts of this section are based on presentation and discussion of a paper by Dr. Joachim Krause on Warsaw Pact CW capabilities.

8. *Report of the Chemical Warfare Review Commission* (Washington: U.S. Government Printing Office, June 1985), p. 26. Hereinafter cited as The Stoessel Report.

9. The Reagan Administration's conclusions regarding Soviet activities on biological and toxin weapons are noted in U.S. Department of Defense, *Soviet Military Power* (Washington: U.S. Government Printing Office, 1986), p. 76.

10. Valerie Adams, "A Retaliatory Chemical Warfare Capability—Some Problems for NATO," *RUSI Journal*, Vol. 130, No. 4 (December 1985), p. 17. Official intelligence estimates of Soviet stockpile size are classified, and it is unclear to what extent they would narrow the range of uncertainty.

11. *Soviet Military Power*, pp. 72–74.

12. Parts of this section are based on presentation and discussion of the Krause paper.

13. Of course, to the extent this argument is true, it begs the question whether a capacity to retaliate against the other side's distant targets would have much deterrent value.

14. *The Stoessel Report*, pp. 19–24.

15. Ibid.

16. Parts of this section are based on presentation and discussion of papers prepared by General Frederick Kroesen (USA, ret.) and Dr. Theodore Gold on NATO's CW priorities and program options.

17. Any munition with area effects will pose risks to civilian populations in a wartime situation. The point pressed by many opponents of the *Bigeye* weapon is the disproportionate nature of that risk to plausible military goals. On the one hand, the forms of shelter that civilians would seek in a conventional conflict would not necessarily protect them from the prompt or residual effects of lethal chemical aerosols or vapors. On the other hand, the expected effects of CW and deep interdiction targets are uncertain. Not only are the costs of delivery much higher compared with battlefield use, protection and decontamination are more likely to be available. Because *Bigeye*'s contribution to deep interdiction operations is only marginal, skeptics argue, its value is hard to justify in view of the risk posed to civilians.

18. Figures supplied by the Military Airlift Command, U.S. Air Force. Precise figures on European reinforcement contingencies are not publicly available.

19. The issues at stake in disputes over Soviet compliance with existing limitations on chemical and biological warfare fall outside the scope of this analysis. However, we are grateful to Elisa D. Harris for a detailed review of current issues and to Walter Slocombe for additional comments on various aspects of this topic at the workshop.

20. NATO implicitly recognizes this position as its own, even though a number of countries in the alliance, including the Federal Republic, accept the Protocol's broader interpretation for themselves.

21. Texts of the Geneva Protocol, the Biological Weapons Convention, and the ENMOD Convention are found in U.S. Arms Control and Disarmament Agency, *Arms Control and Disarmament Agreements, 1980 ed.* (Washington: U.S. Government Printing Office, 1980), pp. 14–18, 124–131, 193–200.

22. Parts of this section are based on a presentation and discussion of material prepared by Dr. Robert Mikulak on the current negotiations on chemical weapons.

23. In August 1986, the British government sought to bridge these two positions by proposing an inspection procedure which provides that a state suspected of noncompliance may refuse an inspection, but only after it offers evidence to substantiate its claim of innocence. Noncooperation in providing such evidence would be considered a violation of the treaty. Soviet officials have indicated that the British proposal may provide a basis for negotiation, but there has been no follow-up to date. For a discussion of the British proposal, see David Dickson, "Britain Offers Plan for Chemical Weapons Verification," *Science*, August 8, 1986, pp. 617–618.

24. The final communiqué of the Reagan-Gorbachev Geneva summit is found in *The New York Times*, November 22, 1986.

25. Parts of this section are based on presentation and discussion of material prepared by Mr. Benoit D'Aboville on the various proposals for a European CW free zone.

26. Parts of this section are based on presentation and discussion of a paper prepared by Dr. Julian Perry Robinson.

# GLOSSARY

| | |
|---|---|
| ATBM | Anti-tactical Ballistic Missile |
| *Bigeye* | A binary air-delivered bomb that produces VX nerve agent. |
| Biological agents | Living microscopic organisms that can be used in weapons to cause death or incapacitation. |
| Blister agents | Chemical agents that injure by blistering (burning) the skin and mucous membranes. |
| BW | Biological warfare |
| BWC | Biological Weapons Convention |
| BZ | An incapacitating psychochemical agent that causes disorientation and temporarily degrades mental activities. |
| CD | Conference on Disarmament |
| CW | Chemical warfare |
| ENMOD | Environmental Modification Convention |
| F.R.G. | Federal Republic of Germany |
| GB (Sarin) | A nonpersistent class of nerve agent that |

|  | attacks primarily through the respiratory system. |
|---|---|
| GD (Soman) | A nonpersistent class of nerve agent that attacks primarily through the respiratory system. |
| HE | High explosive |
| IAEA | International Atomic Energy Agency |
| Incapacitating agent | An agent designed to destroy the combat effectiveness of enemy troops without inflicting permanent injury or death. |
| INF | Intermediate-range nuclear forces |
| Lewisite | A blister agent |
| MRLS | Multiple Rocket Launch System |
| Mustard | A persistent blister agent |
| NATO | North Atlantic Treaty Organization |
| NBC | Nuclear/biological/chemical |
| Nerve agents | Chemical warfare agents that bind acetylcholinesterase, an enzyme of the human body essential to the functioning of the nervous system. These are highly toxic and usually kill very quickly. |
| Nonpersistent agent | An agent that retains its potency on the battlefield from a few minutes to about an hour. |
| NPT | Nonproliferation treaty |
| OSI | On-site inspection |
| Persistent agent | An agent that retains its potency on the battlefield for days up to weeks. |
| SED | East German Socialist Unity Party |
| SRBM | Short-range Ballistic Missile |
| SPD | West German Social Democratic Party |
| Toxins | Nonliving chemical substances produced by living organisms. Toxins can now also |

be produced synthetically by genetic engineering.

VX     A persistent class of nerve agent.

Source: *Report of the Chemical Warfare Review Commission* (Washington: U.S. Government Printing Office, 1985), pp. 102–104.